# WHO NEEDS ME?

by Florence Parry Heide

art by Sally Mathews

Copyright © 1971 Augsburg Publishing House
Library of Congress Catalog Card No. 71-159011
International Standard Book No. 0-8066-1134-0
Manufactured in the United States of America

AUGSBURG PUBLISHING HOUSE
Minneapolis, Minnesota

Mr. Erasmus needs me.
I tell him every single thing he knows.

I take care of him.

I take him everywhere. Otherwise
he wouldn't go anywhere.

He sleeps with me all night
so he doesn't have bad dreams.

My mother needs me.
I am her best friend.

I help
her
every
day.

She likes to have me with her all the time.

My father needs me.

He likes to help me tie my shoes.

He likes to read to me.

He tells me what I want to know.

He likes to carry me.

I am just the right size.

When I am sleeping at night,
he tiptoes in to look at me
to see if I am warm enough.

The mailman needs me.
He knows I wait for him.

When I see him coming,
I open the door
and he gives me the mail.

Otherwise

he would have to put it in the mailbox.

He would rather give it to me.

My little plant needs me.

I water it every day.

I put it in the sun.

The birds need me.

I put pieces of bread

out for them

every day.

The man at the store needs me.
He is happy when I come in.

He says he needs customers,
and I am one.

He helps me decide what to buy.

Mrs. O'Connell next door needs me.

She says
otherwise
who would eat the cookies she makes?

The little boy across the street needs me.

I wave to him
and he waves back.

He always waits
until I wave first.

My bed needs me.

I am the only one who fits it.

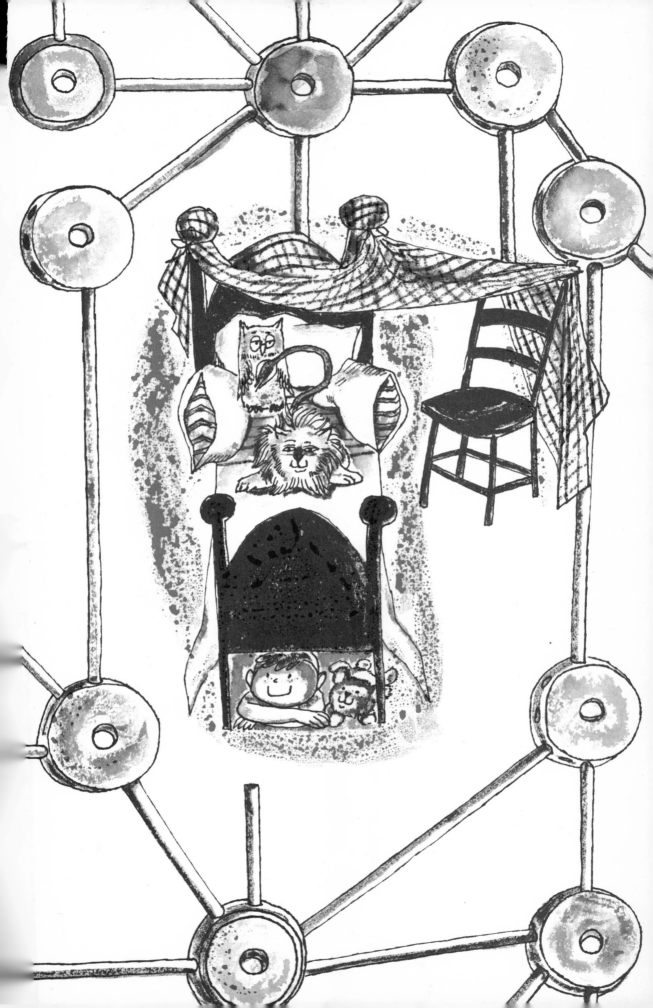

And God needs me.

# A NOTE TO PARENTS

As parents we usually think of our child's need for us. But a child wants to feel needed too. He loves to feel that mother needs him to help or just to be around. He is pleased that father needs him to play with and to read to and to take care of at night.

For the boy in our story, delight in being needed breaks out in daily experiences: his teddy bear needs him; the mailman needs him; his little plant needs him; the birds need him; the storekeeper needs him. The next door neighbor, the boy across the street, his bed, and even God need him.

God needs him? We first think of *our* need for God, and that is proper. We need God—his care, his strength, his love, his forgiveness. And by faith we are confident of his loving care. He has revealed himself in Jesus and told us about himself in the Scriptures.

Yet God also needs us. Our life with him is a mutual relationship. God needs us to praise him, to love him, to serve him, to care for his creation.

You help your child grow as you help him feel needed. A child who feels needed by his family and others around him will be able to accept himself, to feel important, and to feel needed as a child of God.

When you read *Who Needs Me?* with your child, help him talk about how he is needed. And enjoy yourself!